Growing
Up
Three Hollers
from
Lake Wobegon

To: Suellen

My very best wishes
— enjoyed knowing you

Hazel Baker Tudor

June, 2002

Growing Up Three Hollers from *Lake Wobegon*

Hazel Baker Tudor

Meetinghouse Books
Franklin, Tennessee

Printed in the United States of America

05   04   03   02   01   1   2   3   4   5

Library of Congress Catalog Card Number: 2001091853

ISBN: 1-57736-245-4

Cover design by Gary Bozeman

Meetinghouse Books
PROVIDENCE HOUSE PUBLISHERS
238 Seaboard Lane Franklin, Tennessee 37067
800-321-5692
www.providencehouse.com

To my loving children,
Mary, Elizabeth, and John III,
and their spouses,
Nelson Jr. and Dede

and

To my loving grandchildren,
Audra and Adam,
who, as small children,
helped me recall childhood memories with their requests,
"Nanny, tell us more about when you were growing up."

and

In loving memory of my parents,
Gurine and Albert T. Baker.

Contents

Preface & Acknowledgments

On the day of my seventy-fifth birthday, April 3, 1994, I flew to Minnesota to attend Aunt Mina's funeral. She had died at age ninety-seven. The next day, it began to snow during the funeral service. By the end of the burial, the surrounding areas were white and serene, which seemed like the Lord's way of demonstrating the loving and pure life she had led despite the last nine years in the agonizing depths of Alzheimer's disease. By the next morning, it was a winter wonderland, arousing many pent-up memories for me. Since my traveling wardrobe did not include proper attire for this seasonal change, I borrowed galoshes and other warm clothes from my sister and set out to mush through memory lane.

I crossed the highway where we used to imagine seeing Dillinger, the foremost bank robber of that era, in his getaway car. Then it was on past the public school (now a nursing home), and past the chicken hatchery and the blacksmith shop (both no longer in existence). It was at this last place where I remember losing a layer of my tongue. In front was an iron hitching post for horses. During a cold winter day, a friend dared me to stick my tongue on it, which I foolishly did!

When I returned home from Minnesota, some of these memories were documented as *Growing Up Three Hollers From Lake Wobegon*. That was just the beginning of releasing other memorable events about my childhood.

Special thanks to my children, who encouraged me in my writing, and to my teachers, the church, neighbors, and relatives, who all provided much encouragement and love.

Introduction

Dear Mary, Elizabeth and Nelson Jr., John III and Dede, Adam, and Audra,

As we age in life, we tend to become more interested in our heritage and background. Unfortunately for me, I knew very little about my parents except through information given to me later in life by my relatives.

Our lives are shaped so much by our childhood experiences. Therefore, I have written very candidly about my early years with the hope that you can better understand some of my idiosyncracies. This has also been a therapeutic project for me—verbalizing some of my painful memories as well as acknowledging and appreciating the special people in my life who encouraged and loved me. Life leaves many scars; but, like the flaws of antique furniture, they enhance the future value of our lives.

Much love always,
Mom

CHAPTER ONE

Growing Up
Three Hollers from
Lake Wobegon

I grew up in a small Minnesota town which boasted of a covered bridge and fifteen hundred citizens of Scandinavian and German descent, ties to which they were still staunchly allied. Early in my marriage, I crossed the Mason-Dixon line during the beginning of the early 1950s to become a citizen of Music City, U.S.A., known as the originator of the Grand Ole Opry and country music.

Settling into daily living there, my so-called midwestern accent caught the ears of many Nashvillians. I was frequently asked what state I was from. Since the name of my hometown, Zumbrota, had an Indian derivation, it always brought on a puzzled look. I almost sensed that they visualized me as one of those wild rice gleaners in the Indian swamplands. Then miraculously, with the help of Garrison Keillor, Lake Wobegon found its way into popular culture. Hallelujah! Praise the Lord! I now had the answer to my hometown queries! Having learned some of the folklore of the South, I knew that distance was frequently calculated in country style as "so many hollers away." So my pat answer became, "I grew up three hollers from Lake Wobegon." That satisfied their curiosity, and even brought a gleam in some of the men's eyes—those who were familiar with the well-camouflaged home industries that sent up smoke signals of mashed brew in some of those hollers.

As a dream-filled teenager, I yearned and hoped for the day when I could leave the confines of a small town, where one's life was an open book, thanks to the constant clicking on the party lines of the telephone. Now in my advancing years, I am pleasantly nostalgic of those years, realizing and appreciating the many experiences which became the cornerstone of my life.

Life in a small town in that era revolved around the family, the church, and the school. "School keeps today" was always the motto regardless of weather extremes, even when Mother Nature deemed it necessary to help the farmers' moisture level by blowing in mounds of snow. On such days we would enjoy a free ride to school on the rudders of the farmers' sleighs as they hauled the cream to the local creamery. It was an exciting activity—the more the merrier!

I am now convinced that my education was equal to any private school. I vividly remember our English teacher and the methods she used to instill in us the love of Shakespeare. While we were studying *Macbeth*, she chose a portion of it for our class to dramatize in front of the student body. One poignant excerpt became a part of the local scene for many months. When the wicked witch calls out in her crackly voice, "Where hast thou been, sister?" the answer comes from a bevy of teenage boys in their high falsetto voices, "Killing swine, killing swine!" Many of these local Shakespearean actors took an active part in the annual hog killing ritual in the rural areas. So thereafter on many a brisk fall day, one would hear loud and clear, "Where hast thou been, sister?" And from north, south, east, and west, the answers would reverberate and echo through the hollows of the area, "Killing swine, killing swine!" Shakespeare will always live on during hog killing season.

We were blessed with a Carnegie public library. I never knew how a town our size was such a lucky recipient. The librarian lived one door down from our house. She was a large, staid, no-nonsense, erect New Englander who kept house for her aging father. I never did know how she landed in our town, nor did I question it. She was a mentor to me in many ways. Every Saturday during the summer, I would mow her yard for fifty cents plus a candy bar. To me she was the least likely person to be such an avid baseball fan. I can still see the image of her sitting in front of her Atwater Kent radio, loud enough to be heard two houses away. With needle point in hand, she would leap from her rocker and cheer her team to victory. But the real bonus for me was in the realm of her library. She saved all the new arrivals in her literary domain for me. She instilled in me the love of reading for which I have always been grateful.

Halloween was always anticipated with great glee. Palatable goodies were not a part of the scene then. Instead, the pranks we contemplated and carried out would classify us as near delinquents today. But the citizens of the town anticipated and accepted it in their placid way. Half moon outhouses, well equipped with Sears Roebuck catalogues, and unattended farm machinery seemed to be the focus of the pranksters. The morning after Halloween we were up at the crack of dawn to head downtown to view the colorful array of farm machinery lined up on the three blocks of Main Street. By noon every lost item was claimed and school kept as usual.

Since our town had the only covered bridge in the state of Minnesota, it was only right that it had its special day to shine. Memorial Day brought out all the local talent—marching bands, old veterans, local aspiring orators, flower lovers, and lastly the little flower girls chosen to stand in each window of the covered bridge. It was every little girl's dream to be chosen for this honored position. Dressed in a new white dress elaborately sewn by her mother, she would toss a constant stream of petals from her flower basket into the ripples of water below to honor all the soldiers who had perished at sea. In my little girl fantasy, I considered myself as indispensable as Florence Nightingale was to her country. Patriotism has its early roots in childhood and, in solitary moments on Memorial Day, I am still the little girl in that covered bridge window paying homage to our deceased patriots.

When I watched the Winter Olympics in Lillehammer, it brought nostalgic memories of winter shenanigans. One year a heavy rain flooded a nearby creek followed by freezing temperatures, leaving a heavenly skating rink. Only a very exclusive group, the Elites, knew about this three hollers from Lake Wobegon skating arena. We maintained our private arena as long as Mother Nature cooperated. Every evening we skated (do not ask me what happened to school homework), and every evening we ended with the same ritual. Almost unheard of in that era, one of the boys had access to a Ford coupe. After we took off our skates, all eight of us stacked ourselves into the car. Then our intrepid driver would gun the motor out to the middle of the rink, slam on the brakes, and go into a four wheeler Olympic spin. Only the Elites and the Lord knew of this skating benediction.

Progress is inevitable. And with it we lost many of the joys (and sorrows) of everyday, down-to-earth living. But progress cannot eliminate our own special dreams and memories. I am glad I grew up three hollers from Lake Wobegon.

CHAPTER TWO

My No-nonsense Grandfather

My grandfather, Holvor Olson Loken, came to the United States as a young man from Norway, with all the vigor of generations past, to make a new start in the land of plenty. True to the characteristics of the Vikings, he was a stalwart man, not only in his physical dimensions, but also in his temperament.

He worked very hard and did very well in his farm business ventures. Nevertheless, his stubborn nature was not appreciated by his grandchildren, who were "too worldly wise." Eating at his table was a serious matter, and he could not be bothered with superfluous conversation. Consequently, eating at his farm home was one big bore for us. My sister frequently taunted me by pinching me or kicking me under the table, so she could savor the scowls that were directed at me by my grandfather when I resorted to any form of audible complaints.

So we did learn to conform and accept our grandfather's jurisdictions at his table. It also loosened us up for our after dinner ritual of climbing the apple trees in the back orchard. By this time grandfather was taking his after dinner snooze in his horse hair covered rocker. The world was ours!

P. S. I was born on his birthday, so my name, Hazel Leone, corresponds with his initials, H. L.

Grandfather and me.

CHAPTER THREE

My Grandmother Loken

My grandmother, Ambjor Strand Loken, was born in Norway. After her parents migrated to the United States when she was only ten, she was raised by her grandfather, who was a judge. Her mother died four years after coming to America.

My grandmother was a beautiful little girl and, at the age of ten, her portrait was sketched by an itinerant artist Eilif Peterssen who became quite an outstanding man in his field. This original portrait, dated 1870, hangs in the Nesbyen Museum in Hallingdal, Norway.

At age sixteen, she left for America with a small bag of possessions and her spinning wheel. She soon met my grandfather, married him, and settled into primitive farm living. They had ten children, all of whom lived into adulthood except one who died in infancy.

Grandma was a sweet, kind woman who led a typical pioneer life. She had a shy and demure personality, mainly because of the language barrier. Although she understood English very well, she was too embarrassed to speak her broken English (unlike my grandfather). So she communicated to us in Norwegian, while we spoke to her in English.

The only time I remember her using the Norwegian stubborn trait was when my grandparents retired from farm living and built a house in town. Their children had all built successful lives and wanted their parents to have all the modern conveniences. The building went well until my grandmother balked at the electric stove. This upset her farm hospitality ritual. All farm homes had a large coffee pot nestled on the back part of the wood-fueled kitchen range. Whenever a car came into the drive way, this coffee pot was automatically moved to the front to be reheated and served to whomever came into the house. Also the

Grandmother Loken.

range performed a very important part in the Scandinavian culinary ritual. "Lefse," similar to the Mexican tortillas, was baked on the top of a well-polished range surface. So there was an arbitration whereby her old kitchen range was installed in the basement of their new home. As for the coffee, Grandma still adhered to the tried and true hospitality ritual. The result was several coffee pots, forgotten on the front burner of the electric stove, with burned out bottoms.

Life in the "city" (population about 1,500) meant much leisure time, but Grandma learned to adjust. Her hands were never idle. She learned to knit, embroider, and crochet rugs. These rugs were made out of strips of material (old clothes—nothing was ever thrown away) sewn together and rolled into balls. I learned the arts of crocheting and embroidering from her. We spent many happy hours together utilizing these domestic skills. Her knitting projects were given to her numerous grandchildren in the form of mittens. Although my wardrobe was limited, my colorful array of mittens filled a dresser drawer.

I can happily and truthfully say my memories of Grandmother Loken—"Amy" as we sometimes lovingly called her—were warm, both physically and emotionally. She was a loving mentor to me in her subdued and quiet way.

P. S. Family genealogists have traced my grandmother's ancestors to Count Clement and Countess Beljue of Scotland. Move over Henry VIII!

CHAPTER FOUR

Baker Grandparents and Farm Shenanigans

My Baker grandparents, Ole E. Langsbakken and Sigrid Vraalstad Baker, were both born in Norway in the area of Telemark. I did not know as much about these grandparents. When my grandfather came to America, he shortened his name to Bakken. Then at the advice of a neighbor, who suggested he use a more Yankee name, he changed it to Baker.

I never knew my grandfather Baker as he died before I was born. Like many Norwegian migrants, he settled into farming. This same farm, located near Kenyon, Minnesota, is still operated by Baker descendants.

In my very early childhood, my most exciting travel was a yearly train trip (since we had no car) to Kenyon to visit my grandmother. This was only a distance of about fifteen miles, but it probably took close to an hour as we chugged by my other grandparents' farm close enough to wave at them.

Grandmother Baker was a rather sad-faced, white-haired woman who lived in half of the old farm home. She had raised a family of seven children. The other side of the house was occupied by Uncle Ed, Aunt Clara, and their family who operated the farm. Uncle Ed was a jolly, handsome, tall man. Aunt Clara was a patient, loving parent and wife. They had four children close to my age, so these visits were always filled with fun farm activities.

Grandmother Baker's breakfasts were great feasts, always with some sweet ending like cookies or doughnuts. She died at age eighty-five when I was about ten years of age, so my visits ceased after that.

Visiting on a farm meant relying on the utilization of nature's environment for our frivolous fun. A river nearby with a fallen log that covered the width of the stream provided us with a natural swimming pool and jumping board on hot humid days.

My boy cousin, about my age, had captured a raccoon which had its residence in the silo. Our Olympic game then was a "paw fight," putting a cat in the arena with the raccoon, with much cheering from the upper balcony. I do not remember who won the gold medal. But to appease the animal lovers, I can report there was no serious damage other than a few scratches and a high elevation of animal adrenaline.

Another barn activity we enjoyed, provided the operator was on your side, was riding the empty manure hauler a distance of several yards on a high cable. Of course, it ended you guess where—fortunately they were kind to the city girl and never released the dump button!

Even young farm children had certain farm duties. One that I enjoyed was rounding up the cattle for the evening milking. From the surrounding pasture, with the help of a herd dog, we maneuvered the cattle towards the barn. The last half mile was a high hill. My boy cousin eased this climb by grabbing a cow's tail and literally had a ride to the top. I attempted this easy access once, but to be perfectly frank, I was a bit afraid of the back fire. So I huffed and puffed my way up, lagging behind all the rest. For a city slicker, I loved these farm visits. They are still stored in my mind as happy memories.

Baker family.

CHAPTER FIVE

My Father

My father was born in 1880 in Kenyon, Minnesota. He was baptized Ingebrigt Torbjorn but never liked the name, so he changed it to Albert and signed his name as Albert T. Baker.

He graduated from the University of Minnesota Agriculture School in 1901. Shortly thereafter he left for North Dakota, probably because two of his sisters had settled there with their husbands. He acquired over a thousand acres of land through Theodore Roosevelt's Homestead Act. I do not know how he met my mother, but they married in 1906.

Life in that prairie land was rough. I have been told that the winters were so severe that during the raging blizzards a rope was extended from the barn to the house, as there were many tales told of men losing their way even that short distance. Their farm was named Broadview Farm. My father was very fond of horses and had an extensive brood for both travel and farm work.

Medical facilities were very sparse on these prairie farms. All three of us were born at home with the assistance of a midwife. Also of interest is the fact that my sister Molly was stricken with polio at the age of five. She and my mother went by train to St. Louis, Missouri, which was the mecca for polio therapy.

In 1921 my father returned to Minnesota with the purpose of buying land in his home area and returning to live there. As he was en route to the train to return to North Dakota to discuss these plans with my mother, he had a fatal heart attack. I often wonder what my life would have been like, had the medical facilities of today been available then.

My mother moved back to Minnesota, and the farmland was rented and supervised by my Uncle Halbert. This was our only source

Above: Father at Broadview Farm.

Left: My father at Agriculture School.

Mr. and Mrs. Albert Baker and my sister, Almyra, whom we called "Molly."

of income, and during the Depression the income was very lean.

In 1968, long after the death of my mother, the land was sold at a time when farm prices were at a very low level. I was opposed to this, but I was overruled. I had offered to buy the land under the same financial conditions but was told I had selfish motives. My sister Ordelia, whom we called "Dee," who was in charge of the sale, had heart problems. So for the sake of family unity, I relented and forsook my plans. In retrospect it was probably more than I could have managed, but it was hard to give up the land my father had worked so hard to acquire.

I was two years old when my father died—never old enough to experience and know his love. In his memory I can affirm that as a good agronomist, he planted the seeds of his pioneer spirit, and they germinated into a family of survivors.

CHAPTER SIX

My Mother

My mother, Gurine Loken Baker, was born on October 8, 1882. She went by the name of Rena. She attended both a business school and a school of design in Minneapolis, Minnesota. She was a remarkably skilled seamstress as well as in many other areas of handwork. Her silk baptismal and wedding dresses, designed and made by her, were worn by her three children, as well as Mary, Elizabeth, and Audra.

The few possessions I have from her I carried in a treasured box through my many moves—namely pieces of embellished linens and other skilled handwork. For many years, from a decorative viewpoint, they were not in vogue; but how I enjoy them now!

For fifteen years my mother lived the rugged life of a prairie farmer's wife. After my father's death, she and her children moved back to Wanamingo, Minnesota, near her parents' farm. When I was about five years of age, she purchased a house in Zumbrota, perhaps because it was a larger town.

Unfortunately, I have so very few memories of my mother because I was seven years old when she died. The only vivid picture implanted in my mind is being brought upstairs to see her in a room with drawn shades. It was no doubt a deathbed visit. She died of cancer at age forty-five.

The other memory embedded in my mind was the cold day of her funeral. As we were leaving the burial site, I overheard a passing comment: "Look at those poor orphaned children." Perhaps that was the unconscious impetus that pushed me much of my early years to study and succeed, knowing I had no parents to back me.

On Mother's Day for many years, I lovingly wore a white carnation in her memory. Even today, this flower is a symbol to me of a mother's love I cannot remember.

My mother, Gurine Loken.

Above: Loken family.

Left: Three Baker sisters dressed for Mother's funeral.

Mother's funeral.

CHAPTER SEVEN

Aunt Agatha

Aunt Agatha Matilda Loken became our caretaker after my mother's death. It is my presumption that this was a deathbed promise to my mother, so that we three children could grow up together. I rather doubt that we would have been placed in an orphanage, but we may have been parceled out to different relatives as my mother's family was very closely knit.

Aunt Agatha was a tall domineering spinster, about forty years of age when she took over our household. Her homemaking skills were of the highest caliber, but she lacked the qualities of warmth and understanding. She had an unbending personality. Everything was either black or white with no shades of gray.

Her household skills were numerous. She sewed most all of our clothes using the old wrought iron peddle Singer sewing machine. "Boughten" bread was seldom on our table. I remember coming home from school to the welcome aroma of freshly baked bread and sampling it hot with a healthy layer of strawberry jam. Our basement was lined with canned fruits and vegetables, since this was before the era of frozen products. In the fall we harvested apples from our one apple tree. We wrapped each apple in paper and stored them in a big barrel in the cool basement. We also had a vegetable garden, which I wholeheartedly despised since it was my job most of the time to do the weeding.

I never had a room of my own. Since I was the youngest, it fell my lot to sleep in a double bed with my aunt. As a small child I never knew anything different, but as a teenager this became quite troublesome as we had many personality clashes.

We called her "Aggie." Her extremely strict rules became more and more overbearing, since I was a typical teenager who wanted to experience the same activities as my peers. I never saw a movie until I was in high school because a movie theatre was thought to be the "devil's house." Consequently, we would sneak into a movie on the pretense of going to band practice or to the library to study. I remember my first movie very vividly (although it was black and white then). It was *The Trail Of The Lonesome Pine*, starring Henry Fonda and Sylvia Sydney. I came out starry eyed and saw no devils lurking within.

Three sisters.

Dancing was another activity that was prohibited. This rule was very hard to accept, since I had rhythm in my bones. What we now think of as dating was not in vogue then. The one local restaurant was the hang out after a basketball game or studying at the local library. After consuming a ten cent ice cream soda, the gang would break up and, with luck, some boy would ask to walk you home. It was all innocent fun, but Aunt Agatha would be waiting at the door, berating me and my companion. After several such episodes, I would say goodbye to my escort a block from home. Harsh words followed as I entered the house and sometimes my ears were pulled. Many times as a sensitive teenager I cried myself to sleep, and on some occasions crawled under the bed to be alone.

When my two sisters left home for college, we took in three country girls for room and board during the school year. The downstairs library was converted into a bedroom for this purpose. I still did not have a room of my own. This was also during the Depression era, and we were paid in trade, namely farm produce such as milk, eggs, and meat. This period in my life was a blessing for me as I now had three companions, all of whom became my good friends. We even invented a secret code to communicate with each other during the school day.

Keeping up with the fashions.

During the summer months when my sister Dee was home, we occupied the modified downstairs bedroom. When Aunt Agatha had retired for the night, we frequently snuck out to rendezvous with the crowd, again at the only restaurant in town. It was all innocent fun—and what teenager wants to be left out of these social gatherings?

As a busy teenager, I was unaware of Aunt Agatha's complications as a result of menopause. Like all personal subjects, nothing was discussed openly, especially in an all-female household. When I was a senior in high school, it was obvious even to me that something was wrong with Aunt Agatha. That summer she was taken to a rest home in Minneapolis, where she was given shock treatments, the only remedy used for depression in that era. Since she did not respond to this treatment, she was then sent to a mental institution in Rochester, Minnesota, where she ultimately committed suicide by hanging herself with the bed sheets.

I was a freshman in college then. The day of her funeral was one of the most emotional days of my life. After the funeral, which could not even be performed in our church because of their archaic beliefs regarding suicide, I went upstairs at Aunt Mina's house, locked the door, and tried to release all of my pent up and mixed up feelings about Aunt Agatha. I cried bitter tears, not so much over her loss, but over the guilt I felt. All during my childhood I had heard repeatedly, "How lucky you are to have your Aunt Agatha raise you." I was in no position to debate this, so consequently I only swallowed hard.

It took me late into my adulthood to realize how difficult it must have been for a middle-aged spinster to assume the responsibility of raising three children. But she fulfilled my mother's request, and she did her best. It is never too late to say, "I am so very sorry!"

Aunt Agatha with three Baker sisters.

CHAPTER EIGHT

Aunt Mina

Aunt Mina Loken was the antithesis of Aunt Agatha. She was a fun-loving, warm individual who in many ways was really my substitute mother.

She was the second youngest in the Loken family, so when we moved to Wamamingo she was about in her mid-twenties. At that time both she and my Uncle Halbert worked in the local bank. I associate many fun activities with her at my early age. I frequently would walk the railroad tracks with her from Wanamingo to my grandparents' farm for the weekend. Since the town was so small, I was also allowed to walk to the bank to visit my aunt and uncle. One of my favorite activities was to sit on the ledge underneath one of those large bank tables and watch and listen to the money changers.

My bank visit would end when I was given a nickel to spend at the only local grocery store. A nickel's worth of candy went a long way then. On one busy banking day, the usual nickel was not dispensed to me. But my resourceful ears had heard what could be accomplished by simply saying "charge it." So charging five cents worth of candy was easily transacted at the grocery store. The truth was revealed at the end of the month with the charge slip reading, "Baker girl—candy, five cents." My credit came to an abrupt end!

When my grandparents moved to Zumbrota, Aunt Mina was employed at the local bank there and became my grandparents' keeper. Their house was almost directly across the street from our house, so I spent a great deal of time there. My grandfather died when I was about thirteen, so from then on it was only Aunt Mina and my grandmother who lived there.

Aunt Mina Loken.

M Baker Estate

In Account With
J. N. BANITT & SON
Dealers In
GENERAL MERCHANDISE

July	1	Tomatoes			15
"	1	5 ¾ yd. Cretonne ²²		1	27
"	2	Bananas 20 Paid ³⁰			50
"	2	Cocoanut ¹⁵ Tomatoes			25
"	2	3 gal. Kerosene ⁴ ¹⁶			48
"	3	Print 13 Thread ⁰⁵			18
"	3	W. Paper 10 Coffee ⁹⁰		1	00
"	5	6 doz. Buns e.15			90
"	8	Potatoes 30 Prin ⁰⁹			39
"	9	Bread 10 Soap ¹⁰			20
"	9	Lux ¹³ Bananas ⁰⁸			21
"	11	Oil Cloth ⁴⁰ Grapes ¹⁵			55
"	11	Bread			15
"	12	Prin ¹³ Melon ¹⁵			27
"	15	Potatoes ²⁵ Prunes ¹⁸			43
"	15	Wht. Graham			25
"	16	Cod Fish			35
"	16	½ Crate Cherries		1	75
"	16	3 gal Kerosene ⁴			48
"	18	Dish			29

Grocery list.

Aunt Mina was well known in the banking world by the older people because she would do special banking errands for them. She was an avid gardener of both flowers and vegetables. She took care of the yard herself, and continued to use the push mower even when she was in her eighties. Besides being a lover of flowers, she was an antique lover. I easily acquired my interest in antiques from her. She had a special flair with children, and for many years taught a Sunday school class for the kindergarten age group.

When she was in her late thirties or early forties, she learned to drive and purchased a Ford sedan. Since we had no car, she was our chauffeur. She would take us on summer trips to a lake vacation in northern Minnesota. I remember most of all those Paul Bunyan mosquitoes, and the days of itching that followed.

During my troublesome teenage days with Aunt Agatha, Aunt Mina was always there to help and reason with me. Many times after banking hours I would tearfully tap on the window near her work, and she would lead me in and help me through the current dilemma. She was always fair, kind, and loving. She laid the foundation and helped shape my character.

After the death of Aunt Agatha, our house and all its contents were sold. Although my time in Zumbrota was then limited to college vacations, Aunt Mina's house became my home. I even had a room of my own upstairs. My grandmother died at the age of eighty-one, when I was a senior in college.

Aunt Mina continued her work in the local bank until her retirement. It was then she took her trip to Norway, the highlight of which was finding the portrait of her mother in the Nesbyen Museum. She had a photographer make copies for all the grandchildren.

The last nine years of Aunt Mina's life were spent in the local nursing home in the dark despairing world of Alzheimer's. On most of my visits to her she would not recognize me, and frequently would whisper desperately, "I'll give you ten dollars if you'll get me out of here." On my last visit before her death, she had a rare moment when she lucidly said, "Oh, you are Molly's sister, and I am your big aunt. Lean over so I can kiss you."

Her weight dwindled down to less than seventy-five pounds. Death came when, despite her weakened condition, she broke the restraints on her wheelchair. As a result of her fall she broke a thigh bone. Her doctor restricted her to complete bed rest instead of attempting surgery, and she died of pneumonia at the age of ninety-eight.

Death can be kind in this situation. My memories of her are full of happiness and gratitude. I like to visualize her sitting in an antique rocking chair in the middle of a bountiful flower garden, surrounded by singing children—with a push mower available to mow a heavenly lawn.

CHAPTER NINE

Uncle
Halbert Loken

Although Uncle Halbert was not part of my daily life, he, along with Aunt Mina, was one of my legal guardians. He was in charge of overseeing the North Dakota farmland, and he was a very special person to me.

Uncle Halbert was one of the younger Lokens. Except for serving overseas in France during World War I, he lived his entire life in Wanamingo. He was a jovial, fun-loving individual who usually greeted you first with one of his numerous jokes. He was an avid sports lover. He played basketball in high school, and in his latter years would drive to Minneapolis on many occasions to attend the Twins' baseball games. He also dearly loved bird hunting, usually going at least once a year or more to duck or quail hunt in the Dakotas. He had no children as his only child died at childbirth. His wife died at a relatively young age, so he lived the life of a bachelor for many years.

Uncle Halbert was very involved in all the community affairs. He worked in the local bank, later formed his own insurance company, ran the telephone company, and was one of the original founders of the local freezer company. No wonder he was called "Mr. Wanamingo."

Long after I had married and was living in Nashville, I flew to Wanamingo to be Uncle Halbert's nurse after his cataract operation, which was major surgery at that time. One of the first evenings there, I suggested we play gin rummy. With a big grin he replied, "Well, we better pull the shades down!" There was not much excitement in this little town, which was about half the size of Zumbrota. The big social event was the daily visit to the post office to pick up the mail. One

Uncle Halbert Loken.

evening the fire siren rang. I jumped at the opportunity to see some sort of action. Halbert's dole reply was, "Relax, they check out the sirens every Wednesday!"

Uncle Halbert ended his days in the Kenyon Nursing Home. He was lucid to the end, and was the source of much amusement for the nurses with his endless repertoire of jokes, and his innocent desire to occasionally pinch a nurse's derriere.

Despite his lonely life, he was always jovial and a joy to everyone who knew him. He inherited the best of the family genes.

CHAPTER TEN

Christmas, Late 1920s

Unlike the commercialization of Christmas today, with Santa Claus perched in the store aisles shortly before Halloween, Christmas for us did not begin until well after the Thanksgiving holiday.

The first hint that Christmas was just around the corner occurred when I arrived home from school to a house filled with the delicious aroma of Scandinavian baked goods. But we never had a chance to sample them then! They were carefully and meticulously stored in those beautiful tin boxes, now displayed in many antique stores and sold for a king's ransom. But frequently some two-legged little mouse would figure out a way to slip one little morsel out and still not damage the formation—an enjoyable sneak preview!

So the Christmas routine was escalated with fervor. When Christmas Eve finally arrived, many special routines were completed. On this day my grandfather would arrive with an open sleigh to take us to the traditional festivities at my grandparents' farm. It was literally over the river and through the woods, making a path where Mother Nature had thinned out the snow for a suitable road. We were smothered with a horse blanket over our laps and warm bricks at our feet. Grandfather always used the special bells on the horses' harness to supply our Christmas music in the crisp cool winter air.

For a small child, it seemed like an eternity before the farm chores had been completed, and all preparations were ready for the Jule Kveld (Christmas Eve) festive meal. The door to the parlor, where the Christmas tree held forth, was firmly closed and not even a keyhole peek would reveal its contents.

Dressed for snow.

The Christmas Eve meal was never a hurried event, much to the consternation of children eager to open their Christmas gifts. The menu was a replica of what my grandparents had feasted on in Norway. The main entree was "lutefisk," actually cod fish which had been preserved in some sort of a lye solution. It actually tasted as such unless it was covered with an ample supply of drawn butter as well as a rich cream sauce. No one thought of cholesterol or fat content in that nondiet era. Then at long last, the Christmas baked goodies emerged from their stored tin boxes amid the female chatter of who baked what.

The hour had now arrived for the magic door to open. Some Christmas elf, we were told, had lit the candles on the tree. It reflected off the walls, the ceiling, and even off the shiny horse hair covered settee. It was a Christmas fairyland to me—but not for long. The family fire code had to be honored, and each candle was carefully snuffed out. Christmas gifts were scarce in those days, but the love of Christmas was present in the opening of each package as we heard Gladelig Jul (Merry Christmas). After a few Christmas hymns, we were all ready to snuggle down and dream of a white Christmas on which to launch our sleds.

Rural electricity was yet years away, so kerosene lamps were the sole source of lighting. Wood stoves provided the only heat, and the bedrooms upstairs were supplied with heat funneled through small vented openings above these stoves. But in the era before radio or television, the entertainment for rural housewives was quilting, thereby providing down-filled comforters. No wonder we hurriedly dumped our clothes on the floor, and buried ourselves in those downy dunes. And yes, in the morning we somehow managed to get dressed "under the kivvers."

Christmas was certainly different when I was young, but it was still a joyous and religious holiday to store away in my book of memories.

CHAPTER ELEVEN

Me and
Martin Luther

As sure as the sun rose in the east, so was our church attendance where Martin Luther's edicts were devotedly followed. Lands Lutheran Church served mainly the rural community, which was deeply ensconced in the Norwegian traditions. It was about five miles from the town of Zumbrota. For a small church, it had beautiful stained glass windows and an exceptionally good pipe organ.

A great deal of my childhood was spent in organized church activities—Sunday school, youth activities, and choral groups. I credit a great deal of my musical training to our church. I was blessed with a good voice, and this was nourished through organized vocal groups. I sang my first solo at the age of six or seven at our annual Christmas Tree Program. For the occasion I had a newly made blue wool dress, beautifully embroidered by Aunt Mina. But I emphatically refused to wear it because it itched. So a sleeve lining had to be hurriedly implemented for the occasion. At this time of year a beautiful big Christmas tree rose majestically inside the alter ring. Piled high around the tree were Christmas sacks filled with fruit and hard candy, given to the children as they circled the tree. My sister Dee and I always had a contest to see whose candy would last the longest. Sometimes we would hold out on each other until Easter when most of it would be a sticky mess.

As a small child, especially during a Norwegian sermon still given about once a month, it was exceedingly difficult to be well behaved. I must have had an early case of twitchy leg syndrome—for many times a heavy hand was placed on my knees to keep me still. Sometimes I felt as though Martin Luther were lurking right under my pew. I then resorted to counting all the light bulbs, wondering how they were replaced in the high church dome—at one time I could give an accurate figure.

We were never allowed to sit in the balcony for fear of misbehaving. On one memorable occasion when we were guests of a youth group in a Lutheran Church in town, we took full advantage of the balcony seating. On the program was a trumpet solo by a "p. k." (preacher's kid) from that church. He was an excellent musician, but on this particular evening he missed an important high note in his triple tongue ending. We did not need President Bush's advice to "read my lips"—for we easily lip read, "Damn" as he stalked out of the church. The visiting contingency in the balcony had a fun-filled time of tittering and poking each other, and still trying to uphold the Martin Luther standards.

I would like to comment on this family of "p.k.'s." This was a family of five boys all of whom were extremely talented in either art or music. Orville, the oldest son, baptized my daughter Mary in Chicago where he was a pastor of a parish there. He left the ministry to pursue his art studies and later became the head of the art department at Luther College in Decorah, Iowa. Joseph, who sang with me in the St. Olaf Choir, was for several years the organist and choral director at the University of the South in Sewanee, Tennessee. Paul, the youngest, played the tuba in front of me in the Zumbrota High school band and was a real comic. He was on the art staff at Bowling Green College in Ohio. The other two were also heads of college departments. I have original pieces of art done by both Orville and Paul.

Times have altered many of the rigid rules of the Lutheran Church. During one of my visits in the later years, I was pleasantly surprised to hear jazz music played in the church. Although only the older church members recognize me as "one of the Baker sisters," the rural cordiality, still a bit stoic, is ever present. It is interesting to recognize family features in the third generation.

Lands Lutheran Church was a part of many phases of my life—both happy and sad. It is also the place where I can visit my parents' graves and spiritually commune with them. Thank you Martin Luther for my early training and learning of "A Mighty Fortress Is Our God"—your hymn of praise.

CHAPTER TWELVE

Windows '35

The recent advertisements for Microsoft's Windows 95™ advise one to plug into something new. Instead, I look through the rearview mirror of my life and plug into Windows '35. Through this window I see a woman, Mildred Hanson, who plugged new life into me. She was a mighty fortress not only in stature but, like Martin Luther's hymn, she was "my stay what'er doth happen."

Mildred, I politely called her Mrs. Hanson, was bubbly and cheerful, and infused those qualities into making the most menial task a fun-loving challenge. In stature she was about five by five, very neat in appearance, and covered much of her weight with a colorful apron. Her house was immaculate because she had no children or pets, except for a caged canary. But the enjoyment of either of these would have challenged her even more.

I lived one block from her house. During my early teens, Mildred approached me with the idea of helping her with Saturday cleaning. She had no children of her own and knew of my own orphaned status. In retrospect, I see her actions as a loving gesture. But living in my teenage world, I did not see it in that perspective at that time. Instead, it was a business proposition with a monetary agreement.

Until this employment I had known her as a lovable "elder," although she was probably only in her fifties. It did not take long to establish a loving, mothering relationship with her. I was not devoid of any household duties at home, but performing these same cleaning tasks for Mildred took on a different meaning. Dusting her hardwood floors around her rugs on my hands and knees, I found myself humming a happy tune. And hanging her newly washed sheets outside on the line to dry in the era before clothes dryers, I experienced the refreshing aroma of sleeping between those sheets, like lying in a bed of clover.

Another cleaning maneuver common in those days was the semi-annual "airing" and dust battering of large rugs. The battering was performed with a wire rug beater, now a collector's item. On a beautiful fall or spring day, many a housewife savored the swirls of dust and dried food she could strong arm out of these carpets. But Mildred's rugs did not produce billows of dust, somewhat of a disappointment to me.

Mildred's husband was the local auctioneer whose busiest day was Saturday. He had a droll country wit which appealed to all the farmers, who treated all auctions as a not-to-be-missed social event. After a day of his prolonged monologues, selling mainly farm animals and farm equipment, he would come home with muted tongue, and no doubt be blissfully content just listening to Mildred's nonstop recount of her day.

The highlight of the Saturday cleaning day was the tête-à-tête lunch. This was served at a sunny bay window, complete with beautiful china and linen napkins. I was her special guest. The very nature of her honesty and sincerity as she inquired about my school and general activities made it easy to confide in her and find solace for some of my hidden thoughts. I cherished those Saturday cleaning days. I gave my very best performance on those days, but it could not compare with the remuneration I received in return, namely her loving and humble way of instilling me with confidence and self-esteem. Thank you, Mrs. Hanson.

CHAPTER THIRTEEN

Where was Dior?

The fashion magazines of my childhood were the Sears Roebuck and Montgomery Ward catalogs. Since Aunt Agatha was a very unique seamstress, we would pick out a style in one of the catalogues for her to copy. I never had a "boughten" coat until I was a junior in high school. Yet I looked in tune with the times.

My shoe wardrobe consisted of three pairs of shoes per year. In the winter it was high-top laced up shoes, in the summer it was brown sandals, and for dress up it was a similar version of today's Mary Janes. Maybe this accounts for the overabundance of footwear in my wardrobe of today!

In the cold winter we wore a one piece type of union suit which extended to the ankles. Through numerous washings, the elasticity would wear out and become very flabby at the ankles, making it necessary to fold it over under our cotton stockings. Of course it created a look of fat ankles and legs had no shape. Even at that early age, I was vain enough to want to display my shapely legs. So, on the way to school, one block from home behind a neighbor's hedge, I would hoist up my long underwear and bunch them up under my bloomers. As a result, my rear looked a bit out of proportion, but my shapely legs were now very much in evidence. I strode to school a wee bit colder, but vanity was a higher priority.

Later we did have two-piece snow suits, but slacks were not included in the wardrobe of my era. The first style close to slacks that came into vogue one summer were beach pajamas—a one piece suit with legs about a yard wide. I wanted so badly for my aunt to sew me one, but the refusal came that such a style was "too worldly."

Shortly after this refusal, my plight was solved. My cousin from out of town came to visit wearing—lo and behold—a pair of beach pajamas. And her father was a Lutheran minister! Two weeks later, I was parading around in a newly sewn pair of beach pajamas, feeling and looking very worldly. Thank you, Solveig!

My first pair of true slacks was the band uniform. Everyone in the band wore white slacks, over which Aunt Agatha shook her head and rolled her eyes. With our capes and triangular caps, we were a colorful group, even though we may not have been up to John Philip Sousa's musical standards.

Hair styling took on various home mechanics. Crimping the hair was done by heating a curling or crimping iron in a kerosene lamp. Of course, it also resulted in some singed hair. The first permanent wave machine resembled an electric chair. Individual rollers were pulled down from one huge machine while you sat in the middle. The current was then plugged in, and within twenty to thirty minutes you were blessed with curls. My hair genes were straight and fine, so I adored the Shirley Temple look.

The heavily corsetted and girdled women of my mother's era would turn over in their graves now at the hatless women with too much skin showing. The Madonna they admired was not the Madonna of today.

This Granny cannot resist mentioning her old philosophy that it is "what's inside that counts." This is not a new philosophy. I quote Johann Wolfgang von Goethe, who wrote in 1806, "You are in the end—exactly what you are. Put on a wig with a million curls, put on your feet the boots with the highest heels, yet you remain in the end just what you are."

CHAPTER FOURTEEN

The Flavor of Zumbrota

T he flavor of Zumbrota could best be described as vanilla, generously topped with honesty, loyalty, helpfulness, and thriftiness—most often served over a chatty cup of coffee. There were few nonconformists.

This was the porch-swinging era prior to air conditioning. At the end of a hot day, these swings were a cooling oasis before going to bed. Sometimes on very hot evenings, we would bring our blankets and sleep in the front yard, which was surrounded by a hedge. Most telephones operated on a party line, whereby any person could listen in on the conversation. Needless to say, between this easy access to neighborhood news and the evening watch on the porch swings, there was not much privacy—gossip has always been enjoyed in any generation.

Phenomenal changes have occurred since I was a young girl. We did not have dishwashers, clothes dryers, electric blankets, credit cards, ballpoint pens, panty hose, Xerox, penicillin, plastic wares, tape decks, yogurt—everyone made do with what they had. No one ever dreamed that a human would set foot on the moon!

There was one grocery store in town, which was really a mini department store. One side accommodated the food supplies, and the other side had dry goods such as sewing supplies, and a few basic clothing items. Upstairs in a little cove was a millinery department, as hats were essential for churchgoing females.

I was frequently assigned to do the grocery shopping. Each item on my grocery list was brought to the counter by the clerk. Basic items such as sugar, flour, and salt were stored in large wooden bins and were measured out on a huge scale. I remember well the wooden vats that contained the lutefisk that was much loved by the loyal Scandinavians. It never smelled very edible, though. There was also a telephone ordering system. The groceries were delivered by a neighbor with a type of horse-drawn covered van. I am not sure who paid for this service.

The meat market was a separate store. I loved going in there during the hot summer months as the floor was carpeted with soft, moist sawdust, which was soothing to my bare feet. At that time, hamburger was ten cents a pound, and liver and soup bones were gratis. On one of my routine visits there, I heard a beautiful woman at the counter requesting in a southern drawl, "I want fowe poke chops please, Sir." Having heard only the Norwegian and German dialects, and never having heard anyone addressed as "Sir," my curiosity was immediately aroused. When I learned of her identity as the new doctor's wife, I was even more jealous of her beauty and status. It had taken only one legitimate visit to this handsome, young physician's office for me to be smitten with my first teenage crush. On numerous occasions, I tried to simulate illness in order to revisit his office—but to no avail. Prior to this physician establishing a new office in Zumbrota, we had been treated for years by an elderly, obese, asthmatic, wheezing doctor whose office was in his own home.

In that era many illnesses were treated by age-old natural home remedies. Bronchial coughs were treated by placing a hot onion poultice on my chest. It not only had a repulsive odor but frequently left a red burned area. The only illnesses I recall having were shingles and yellow jaundice, now called hepatitis. I do not recall that I even missed school days for these maladies.

I cannot honestly rave about the culinary arts of my childhood except for the sweets and the bread. Most of our food staples consisted of locally grown fruits and vegetables and meat during the fall butchering season. Meat was either canned or dried. It has often been noted that the frugality of the area was so dutifully observed that during the hog killing season, only the squeal of the pig went unused. It was frequently my duty, not by choice, to assist with one of these "waste not, want not" endeavors. For my readers with sensitive stomachs, I suggest that you use your own imagination regarding what these duties consisted of and skip the following episode. However, curiosity often gets the better of us, so continue reading at your own risk.

The blood of the pig was not thrown away but made into "blod polse" (blood bologna). The blood was boiled in a large vessel with flour and suet. After it had thickened, it was spooned into long narrow tubes made from flour sacks (flour frequently came in muslin sacks that were used in numerous ways). My job was to hold these muslin tubes as the mixture was spooned into them. Needless to say, I did this with my eyes closed. After it had been slowly boiled again in the tube, then cooled and congealed, it was cut into slices, fried, and served for breakfast. I'm sure my children were happy that I did not keep this recipe!

There was no social security and, as a result, especially during the Depression years, there were many transients whom we called hobos. Many were train hoppers who managed to survive by going from house to house begging for food. We never turned one away and would serve them a sandwich or leftovers on the back porch. Word seemed to get around among this group that certain families were generous with handouts—by way of a secret code system that we could never figure out—and hobos routinely appeared at our home asking for food. For the most part, these were harmless individuals. Homes were seldom locked, and no one seemed to worry about violence or theft.

Most of our entertainment consisted of outdoor activities. In the spring when the snow had melted, the neighborhood gang would gather on a nearby vacant lot for softball. We also played hopscotch, skipped rope, had yo-yo contests, and roller skated from one end of the town to the other—a total of several blocks. We also played "Annie, Annie, Over." The gist of it was to throw a softball over a house (the bigger the house the better) to a receiver on the other side as we yelled, "Annie, Annie, Over." Whoever caught it scored a point.

Although we lived in the land of ten thousand lakes, we did not have one in our area. The boys would gravitate to the gravel pit for their swim, but for moral reasons the girls were not welcomed there. That accounts for my not being an Olympic swimmer!

We had long winters for plenty of skating, skiing, and sledding. After pursuing these activities, we would warm ourselves by lying on the floor with our frigid feet propped up on the warm radiators—and fortifying our bodies with hot chocolate.

Since this was long before we even imagined such a thing as television, we enjoyed radio programs. I recall running home from school in time to hear my favorite program, "Jack Armstrong, The All American Boy." We played games such as pit and dominoes—but never on Sunday—unless we played it secretly under the bed covers.

In the summer months, the Wednesday night band concert was a big social event, and it was also a boon to the merchants who remained open. Most Wednesdays the great Zumbrota High School band was featured on a large bandstand in the middle of Main Street. I boom-boomed through many Sousa marches on the great walkway. It was an evening for the farmers to discuss their crops, and the cooped-up farmers' wives to enjoy the enchantment of city life.

The Loken family was a closely knit group. I loved visiting my cousins on the farm. Thrashing days were memorable events. All the neighboring farmers would combine their efforts and help each farmer during this season. We loved riding on the bundles of grains stacked high up on the hay wagons. I marvel now at my relatives who put up with extra children during this busy event. All the men were served meals. The cooking was done over hot stoves and served on big tables in the farm lawn.

Fourth of July was usually a big family gathering in a farm pasture bordering a river. The men played horseshoe, and the children waded in the river, boasting about who had been invaded with the most blood suckers. The food was bountiful, and usually someone made ice cream. I was blessed with caring relatives, all of whom did their part in making our parentless life more pleasant.

Over the years, modern technology has changed the flavor of Zumbrota. But the old flavor, which I knew, will never be altered in my mind or heart.

CHAPTER FIFTEEN

School Days, School Daze, Dear Old Golden Rule Days

The Golden Rule was truly upheld during my school days. Teachers were authoritarians whom we seldom questioned. To be issued a summons to go to the principal's office created terror in our hearts. In other words, we respected the discipline imposed upon us in school. Many of Norman Rockwell's *Saturday Evening Post* covers were reminiscent of this era.

I went through all twelve grades in the Zumbrota school system. I thought my first grade teacher Miss Nichols was an absolute beauty. Although all my teachers could not be classified as Miss Americas, I do not recall disliking any of them. They all instilled in us the importance and joy of learning and achieving.

Extra curricular activities were high on my list, and I delved into many of them—some better than others. Music was one of my priorities, being a part of both the glee club and band. I had inherited musical tendencies—my father played the violin, and his sister taught piano when she was not tending her millinery store.

Beginning in the first grade, the music teacher would bring to our class a portable victrola. I remember very vividly how she helped us musically visualize the trolls romping around in Grieg's "In the Hall of the Mountain King." By the time we were in the third grade, we began learning how to read music.

In one of the lower grades, I was in a recital with a girlfriend. She gave a piano recital, and I sang several solos. Since her uncle was the editor of the local paper, we even had a beautifully printed program. How much more important could we be!

When I was in the sixth grade, my teacher was also the band director. I must have tapped my feet overzealously, for he recognized

The bass drummer, Zumbrota High School.

Piano Recital

Given by
MISS JANE HOCKENBERGER

Assisted by
MISS HAZEL BAKER

Song of the Aspen Leaves ....Crawford

Danse Caprice .... Grieg

Song .... "Little Moon"
Miss Hazel Baker

Po Ling and Ming Toy ....Friml
1—Po Ling and Ming Toy
2—A Chinese Love Song
3—Time O'Gloaming
4—Cometh as a Bride

Song ...."A Little Prayer"
Miss Hazel Baker

By the Brook ....Boisdefre

Khaki and Blue (March) ....Adams

Piano recital program.

that I had good rhythm—he asked me to be the bass drummer in the band. In the marching band, I was a bit small to carry the big drum by myself. I had a boy classmate help carry the drum in front of me when it was strapped onto my back. This was most helpful except when he occasionally would get out of sync with the beat, and my stomach would bear the brunt of a bobbled drum. The band played at football games, basketball games, and led the annual parade on Memorial Day to the Veterans Memorial Cemetery. (On a recent visit to Zumbrota on Memorial Day, I witnessed this same ritual— except the band was three times as big with three bass drummers.)

I loved and participated in all sorts of sports activities—softball, field trials (I did pole vaulting), and basketball. We did not have a school gym, so all games were played in the armory on Main Street. I loved basketball, and was an aggressive forward. This was in the era of three guards and three forwards per team, dividing these players by the center line. The forwards awaited eagerly on this line for the

My graduation picture.

guards to retrieve the ball and pass it to us. Since none of the players were exceptionally tall, my favorite shot was the bank board shot. Women were not allowed to compete with other schools, so this was an intramural organization. I can boastfully report that I made the all-star team as a freshman.

Since the boys played other neighboring schools, we loved being a part of the cheering section. Like Zumbrota, many schools did not have gymnasiums. When our team played in Wanamingo at the Veteran's Hall, the players had to be very agile to avoid running into a hot coal stove bordering the baseline.

My love of sports also included developing crushes on the good athletes. This situation led me to help our star quarterback with his math after school hours. His mother was deceased and his father was an alcoholic. I guess that was the beginning of my social work career.

HAZEL BAKER
Valedictorian

Boom, boom, boom! Here she comes! The bass drummer of the school band, Hazel Baker. The Zumbrota school has a loyal and faithful follower in Hazel, for she has at-

I was valedictorian of Zumbrota High School.

We walked to school and also went home for lunch. I was a late sleeper, and many mornings I had to make a wild dash to get there on time. We were never considered late as long as we were in the classroom before the bell quit ringing. I know the janitor helped me many a morning by pulling the rope longer than normal. Also in the spring with the melting snow creating little streams in the gutters, it was quite normal to see us all slushing home in these rivulets.

Our fire escape system was quite unique. On each side of the school building was a tubular covered slide from the second floor to the ground. We loved the fire drills zipping down the tube—one in particular which had a bend in the middle. The boys were especially delighted when asked to be the "catchers" at the bottom. This was before the girls wore slacks, so the wind velocity created by this performance ballooned up all the skirts much to the delight of the

Hello, St. Olaf College!

opposite sex. Some of the more prudish girls would cross their legs, and the devilish catchers would delight in letting them land on their derrieres.

I can honestly say I enjoyed school. I had many friends, and mixed well with all of them. Because I did not have parents to support me, my competitive spirit always spurred me on to succeed and win. This apparently was an inherited trait with all three of us girls, as we all graduated as valedictorians. Of course competition was not too big a factor in a class of about thirty-two students.

On June 10, 1937, I graduated from Zumbrota High School. So with the strains of "Pomp and Circumstance" ringing in my ears and pulling at my heartstrings, I sadly and proudly waved goodbye to growing up three hollers from Lake Wobegon. Thanks for the memories!

CHAPTER SIXTEEN

Is Nostalgia Senseless?

The younger generation may view nostalgia as senseless. But for people who are in their vintage years, nostalgia is frequently a vivid reality precipitated by the various senses, such as touch, taste, smell, hearing, or sight. As senior citizens, we may complain about loss of memory, notably of recent events, but our numerous senses can reactivate and very clearly stimulate valuable memories of the past, and we are happily immersed in nostalgia.

Regardless of the shape of our noses, their function can trigger many memories. A waft of freshly baked bread can take me back to the 1930s. Then I recall breathlessly arriving home from school to Granny's kitchen. Soon my face is shamelessly smeared with strawberry jam after consuming one or more slices of freshly baked bread. Granny is proudly and contentedly enjoying my gourmet plunder as she clicks her knitting needles, creating more colorful mittens for my already flourishing warm wardrobe. Such memories can never be senseless!

Can a perfume trigger an old memory? I did not think they could for me! The lavish, exotic, sexy, and stylized perfumes of today have never produced an aromatic high for me. But one evening as I was idly meandering about in an antique mall, the hair in my nostrils suddenly stood on end—could it be after all these years? Turning my nose in the air, I prowled my way through the crowd like a labrador on the trail of a duck. My well-trained nose led me literally to Blue Horizon—there on the counter was the Evening In Paris complete toiletry set encased in its original blue velvet lining! Suddenly I was in an old dreamworld in the arms of my first love as he gifted me with love and affection. In an absolute trance I choked out, "Yes, I would love to go to the prom with you!"

"You'll do what?" shouted the bewildered clerk behind the Blue Horizon counter. Back to reality, I blushingly replied, "Oh I would love to buy the Evening In Paris set," without even asking the price, which was quite unlike me. My Evening In Paris at the mall was a million-dollar nostalgic memory! Senseless? Not for me!

Somehow the sounds on a cold, clear night are more acute in the wee small hours of the morning, especially when I succumb to occasional sleeplessness during those hours. A train whistle sounds so lonely that I find myself empathizing with the engineer. I then mesmerize myself into reliving my early train rides to my grandparents' farm. This was only a distance of about fifteen miles, but the train chugged along for an hour through beautiful farm country. Farm activities for a city girl were a newfound experience.

Yes, nostalgia makes a great deal of sense. Like the flaws and uniqueness of antiques, these golden memories enhance the value of our lives.

Loken family reunion.

CHAPTER SEVENTEEN

My
Independence
Day

As a senior citizen, the years have seemingly rolled along too quickly. I find the events of the past are so much more vivid and poignant, almost blotting out the daily details of today or yesterday. Nostalgia reigns!

With each approaching celebration of the Fourth of July, precious memories flood my soul. Independence Day in my small hometown of fifteen hundred patriotic citizens brought out a marching band, several stalwart war veterans, and the rest of the town's citizens patriotically waving their American flags. But what I treasured most was the annual family gathering on this day. On this historical event, I have become lost in a trance of happy memories.

The setting for this family gathering was in the rural pastures of my aunt and uncle. It was a perfect environment for every generation—with a bubbling river for the children to explore, a vast flat area for the men to play horseshoe, and a shaded area for the women to set up and display their culinary skills and trade recipes.

Since I was known as the town girl, I became the brunt of many of my cousins rural pranks, but not with malice. I learned much of the country lore over the years—where to find the four-leaf clovers and how to swing off a rope and plop into the swimming hole below. At a close distance was a herd of cows placidly eyeing us, but not too happy over our usurping their watering hole. As one energetic bovine attempted to reclaim her territory, the other matronly companions surrounded her and lured her back to their grazing area as though honoring the frivolity of the day.

After emerging from the water after two or three hours of horse-play and water pranks, the contest began on the banks of the river as to who received the prize of having acquired the most blood suckers. I was told it was a sign of "good blood." At first these slimy creatures almost clogged up my gastrointestinal tract, but I eventually learned the tricks of not allowing them to rest in peace between my toes. One year I even earned the first prize—namely an extra scoop of home-made ice cream.

The men by this time had announced the diamond king of the horseshoe tournament, albeit with a bit of rural language behind the backs of their better halves. The women had swapped recipes and exchanged the local gossip heard on their rural party-line telephones.

By now the picnic tables displayed an array of gourmet delicacies. In that era gourmet meant good old country cooking. And that it truly was with no concern over high calories or high cholesterol. Everyone ate heartily of freshly fried chicken (their heads had been wrung that morning), potato salad, deviled eggs (laid the day before), and all-night baked beans.The final touch was the exhaulting and tempting array of homemade pies and cakes, topped off with freshly churned ice cream. This was truly a country gourmet spread.

After loosening their belts and expressing thanks to the Lord for the bounties of the year, and fondly bidding everyone farewell, all the families disbanded to their respective farms to complete their rural evening duties.

But this town girl went back to her urban home where she wearily sank into the porch hammock. With the full moon emerging in the twilight sky, the summer breezes gently swaying my hammock, and the haunting song of the night owl, I was pleasantly lulled to sleep. In the twilight of my sleep would come the grateful revelation, that despite being left parentless at the age of seven by the early death of both parents, and being left in the care of a spinster aunt, I learned the real meaning of Independence Day. This day was always a reminder of the gentle and protective concern my family relatives displayed the other three hundred sixty-four days of the year as well. As the years progressed, it became the dawn of my independence.

About the Author

Hazel Baker Tudor was born in Lawton, North Dakota. She grew up in Zumbrota, Minnesota, where she and her two sisters were raised by extended family after the untimely deaths of their parents. After graduating as valedictorian from Zumbrota High School, Ms. Tudor attended St. Olaf College, where she received her bachelor's degree in sociology and physical education and sang for four years in the St. Olaf Choir, under the direction of F. Melius Christiansen. She later earned a master's degree in medical social work from Case Western University.

Following her career as a medical social worker in Iowa, she served as president of the Davidson County Medical Auxiliary and as a board member of the Nashville Mental Health Board, the Monroe-Harding Children's Home, and the Florence Crittenden Home. She is a member of the Centennial Club and an elder at Westminster Presbyterian Church.

Ms. Tudor currently resides in Nashville, Tennessee, where she works as an antique dealer. She has three grown children and two grandchildren.